De-Lovely

Project Manager: Jeannette DeLisa
Music Arranged for the Motion Picture by Stephen Endelman
Project Coordinated by Jonathan Watkins for MGM Music
Songbook Design: Martha Lucia Ramirez

CONTENTS

IT'S DE-LOVELY

Words and Music by
COLE PORTER

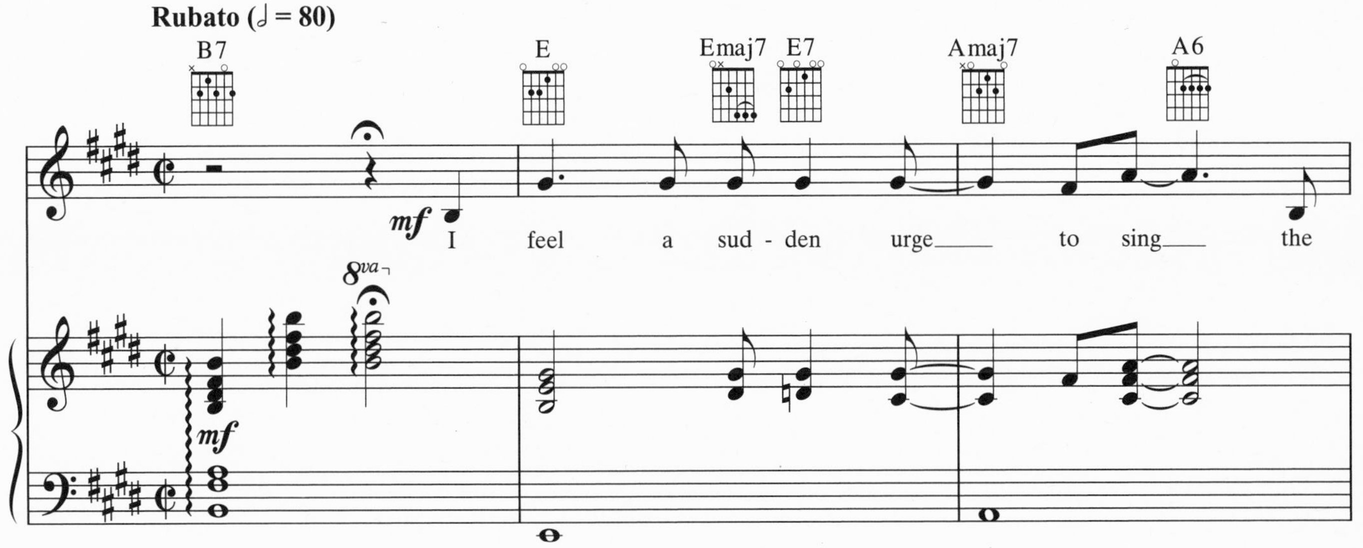

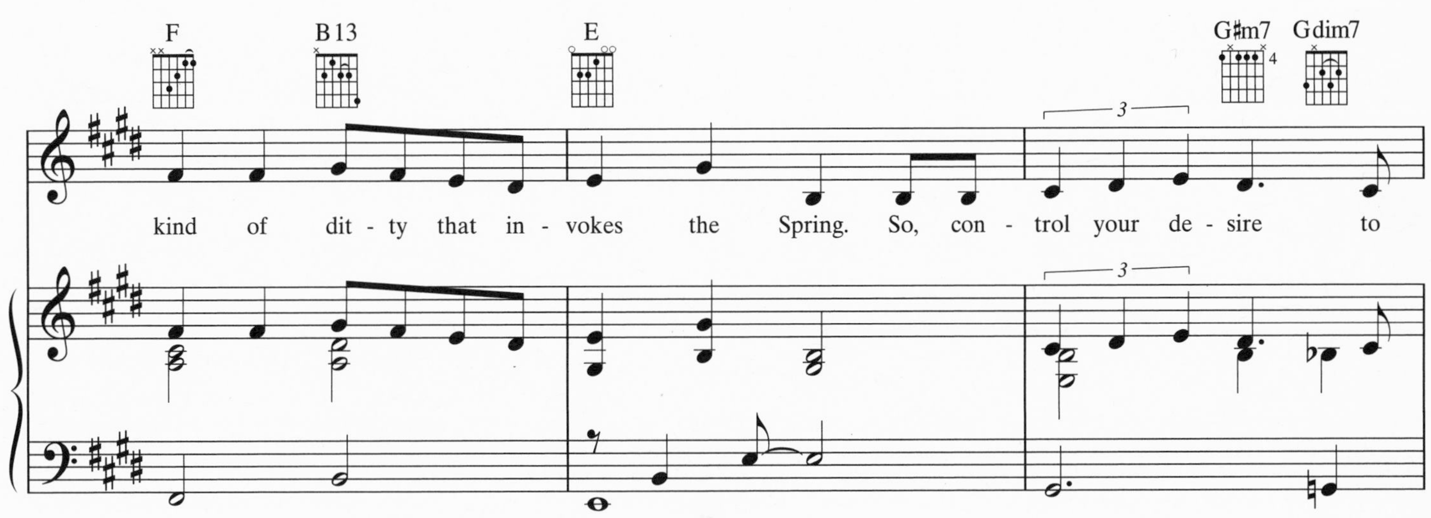

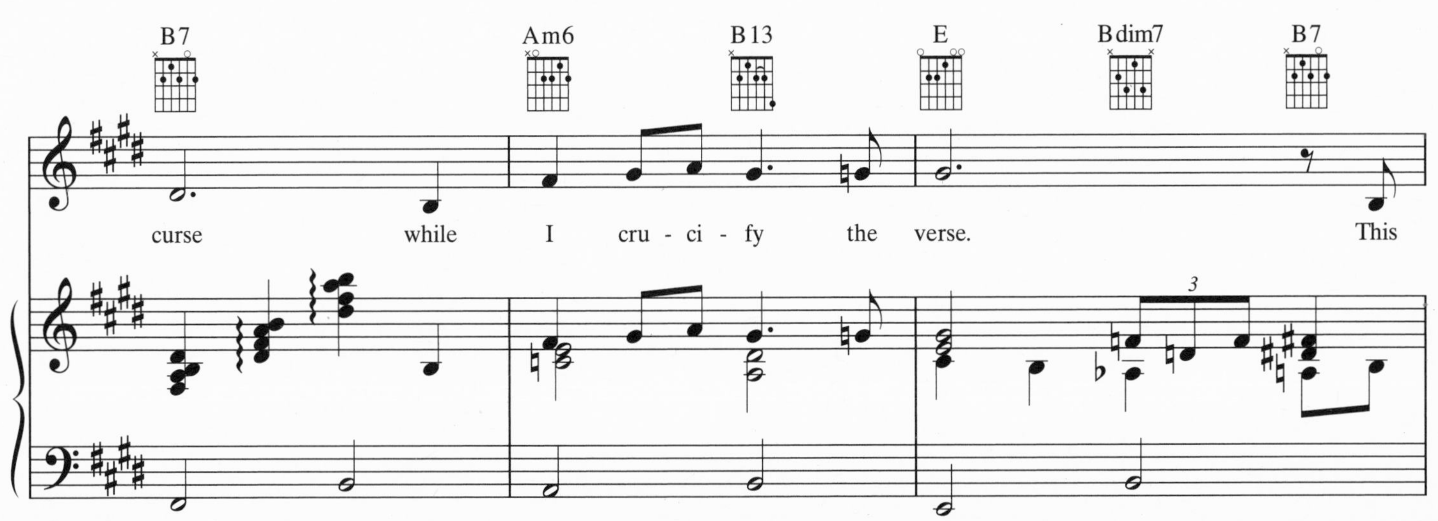

E
Emaj7
E7
Amaj7
A6
B7sus
B13
verse you've start - ed seems to me the Tin Pan - ti - the - sis of
E
C♯m7
F♯7
Bmaj7
B6
mel - o - dy. So, to spare you all the pain, I'll
G♯7
C♯m7
Gdim7
F♯7
B7
B/F♯
skip the darn thing and sing the re - frain. Mi, mi, mi, mi.
A/E
G/D
B7
Re, re, re, re. Do, sol, mi, do, la, si. Take it a-way!

Bright swing ♩ = 80 (♫ = ♩ ♪ triplet)

E Gdim7 F♯m7

B7

Verses 1 & 3:

E E+

1. The night is young, the skies are clear, so
(3.) knot is tied, and so we take a

E6 Emaj7 E

if you want to go walk-ing, dear, it's de - light - ful, it's de -
few hours off to eat wed-ding cake. It's de - light - ful, it's de -

Fdim7 B7

li - cious, it's de - love - ly. I
li - cious, it's de - love - ly. It

F♯m
D/F♯
F♯m6
un - der - stand the rea - son why you're sen - ti - men - tal, 'cause
feels so fine to be a bride, and how's the groom? Why, he's
F♯m7
Gdim7
so am I. It's de - light - ful, it's de - li - cious, it's de -
slight - ly fried. It's de - light - ful, it's de - li - cious, it's de -
E6
F♯m7
B7
E7sus
love - ly. You can tell at a glance
love - ly. To the pop of cham - pagne,
E9
A
what a swell night this is for ro - mance. You can
off we hop in our plush lit - tle plane till a

Am7
D7
G
hear dear Moth - er Na - ture mur - mur - ing low,
bright light through the dark - ness co - zi - ly calls,
B7sus
B7
E
E+
"Let your - self go." So, please be sweet, my chick - a - dee, and
"Ni - ag - 'ra Falls." All's well, my love; our day's com - plete.
E6
Emaj7
E
when I kiss you, just say to me, "It's de - light - ful, it's de -
What a beau - ti - ful brid - al suite. It's de - ream - y, it's de -
Emaj7/D#
E7/D
C#7
li - cious, it's de - lect - a - ble, it's de - li - i - ous, it's di -
rows - y, it's de - rev - er - ie, it's de - rhap - so - dy, it's de -

F♯m11
B7
F♯m11
To Coda
lem - ma, it's de - lim - it, it's de - luxe, it's de - love - ly."
re - gal, it's de - roy - al, it's de - Ritz, it's de - love - ly.
Verse 2:
E N.C.
E
E+
2. Time march - es on and soon it's plain, you
E6
Emaj7
E
won my heart and I've lost my brain. It's de - light - ful, it's de -
Fdim7
B7
li - cious, it's de - love - ly. Life

F♯m
D/F♯
F♯m6
seems so sweet that we de - cide it's in the bag to get
F♯m7
Gdim7
un - i - fied. It's de - light - ful, it's de - li - cious, it's de -
Slower, in four ♩ = 104
E6
F♯m7
B7 N.C.
E7sus
E9
love - ly. See the crowd in that church. See the
A
Am7
proud par - son plopped on his perch. Get the sweet beat of that

D7
G
B7sus
B7
or - gan, seal - ing our doom;
"Here goes the groom." Boom!
A tempo 𝅗𝅥 = 80
E
E+
E6
How they cheer and how they smile as we go gal - lop - ing
Emaj7
E
Emaj7/D♯
down the aisle. "It's di - vine, dear, it's di - veen, dear, it's de -
E7/D
C♯7
F♯m11
wun - der - bar, it's de - vic - tor - y, it's de - val - lop, it's de - vin - ner,

B7sus
E
D.S. 𝄋 al Coda
it's de-voiks, it's de - love - ly.
3. The
Coda
E
Rubato, half as fast (♩ = 80)
We set-tle down as
E+
E6
Emaj7
man and wife to solve the rid-dle called mar-ried life. It's de-
Fdim7
B9sus
E(9)
rit.
light - ful, it's de - li - cious, it's de - love - ly.
rit.

EV'RY TIME WE SAY GOODBYE

Words and Music by
COLE PORTER

B♭/D
D♭dim7
Cm7
F7
B♭7sus
B♭7
E♭maj7
E♭6
why the gods a - bove me, who must be in the know
E♭m6
D♭maj7
D♭6
C7
F7sus
F7
think so lit - tle of me, they al - low you to go.
...end solo)
B♭
Gm9
B♭
Gm9
B♭
Bdim7
Cm7
G♭7
F7
(1.2.) When you're near, there's such an air of spring a - bout it,
B♭maj7
Cm7
D♭maj7
Cm11
F7/C
B♭
B♭7
E♭maj7
A♭7(♯11)
I can hear a lark some - where, be - gin to sing a - bout it.

1.
2.
B♭/D D♭dim7 F7/C F7 A♭/B♭ E♭maj7 E♭m
There's no love song fin-er, but how strange the change from ma-jor to mi-nor,
Dm G7 C7sus C7 F7 A♭/B♭ E♭maj7
ev - 'ry time we say good - strange the change
Rubato
Slower
E♭m Dm7 G7
from ma - jor to mi - nor, ev - 'ry time
a tempo
C7sus C7 F7sus(♭9) F7 B♭ Gm9 Cm9 F13 B♭
we say good - bye, good - bye.
molto rit.
a tempo
rit.

JUST ONE OF THOSE THINGS

Words and Music by
COLE PORTER

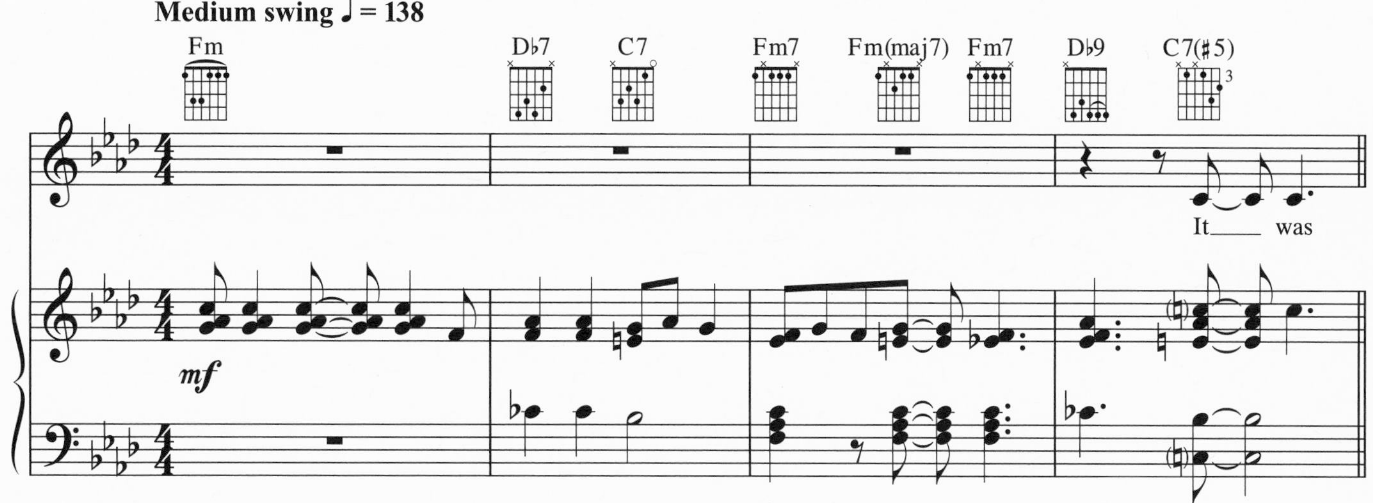

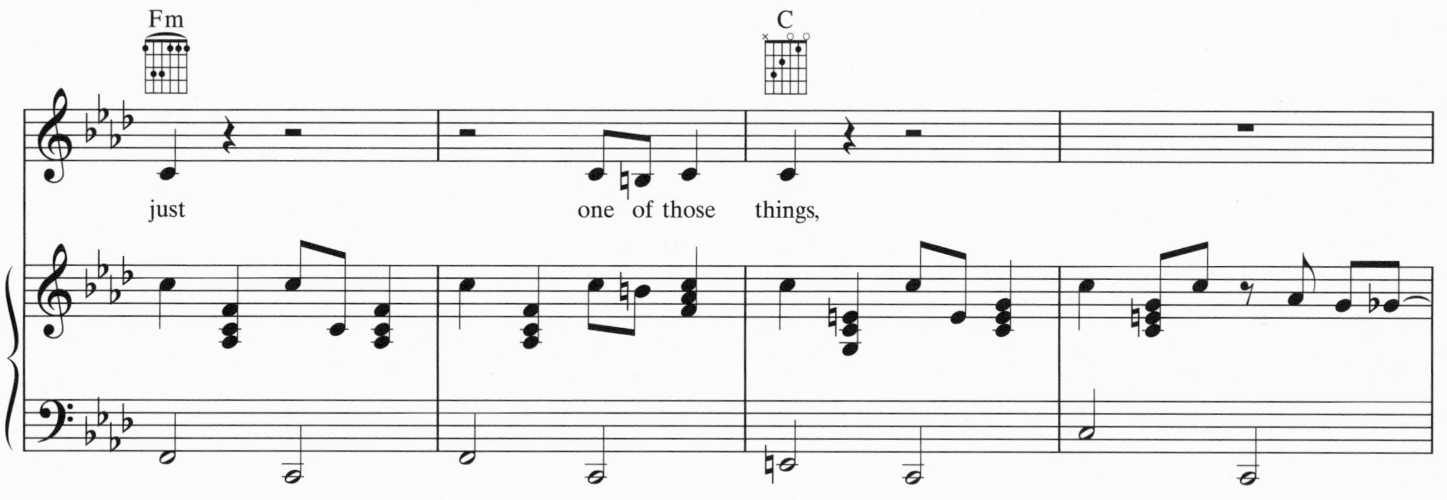

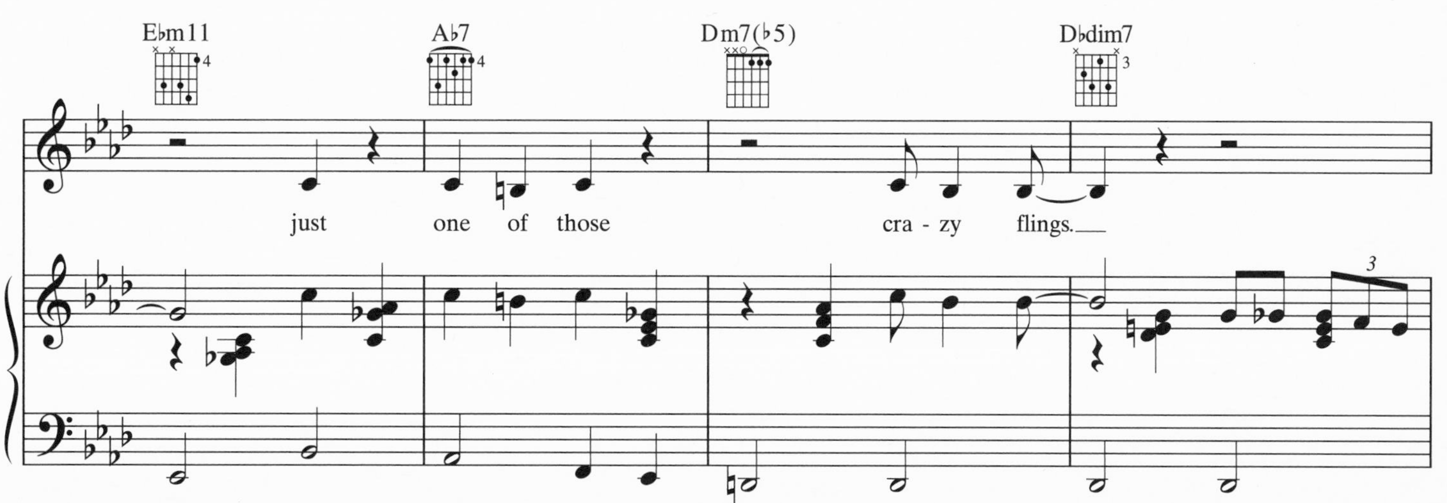

Cm7
Fm7
B♭m7
E♭7
One of those bells that now and then rings,
A♭maj7
F7/A
B♭m7
C7
Just one of those things. It was
Fm
C
just one of those nights,
E♭m11
A♭7
Dm7(♭5)
D♭dim7
just one of those fab - u - lous flights.

Cm7
B dim7
B♭m7
E♭7
A trip to the moon on gos - sa - mer wings,
Cm7
B dim7
B♭m7
D♭13
just one of those things. If we'd
G♭maj7
A♭m9
D♭7
thought a bit of the end of it when we
G♭maj7
B7
Fm7
B♭7
start - ed paint - ing the town, we'd have

Cm
Cm7/B♭
Am7(♭5)
A♭m(maj7)
A♭m7
been a - ware that our love af - fair was too
Gm7
G♭dim7
Fdim7
E13
C7(♯9)
hot not to cool down. So good -
Fm
C
bye, dear, and A - men.
E♭m11
A♭7
Dm7(♭5)
D♭dim7
Here's hop - ing we'll meet now and then, It was

Cm7
F7
B♭m11
great fun but it was just
1.
E♭13
A♭maj7
D♭13
Cm7
F7(♭9/♯5)
B♭m7
F7
one of those things.
Gm7
C7(♯5)
2.
E♭13
N.C.
D♭maj7
It was one of those things.
Cm7
B7
B♭m7
A13
A♭maj13(♯11)
poco rit.

BE A CLOWN

Words and Music by
COLE PORTER

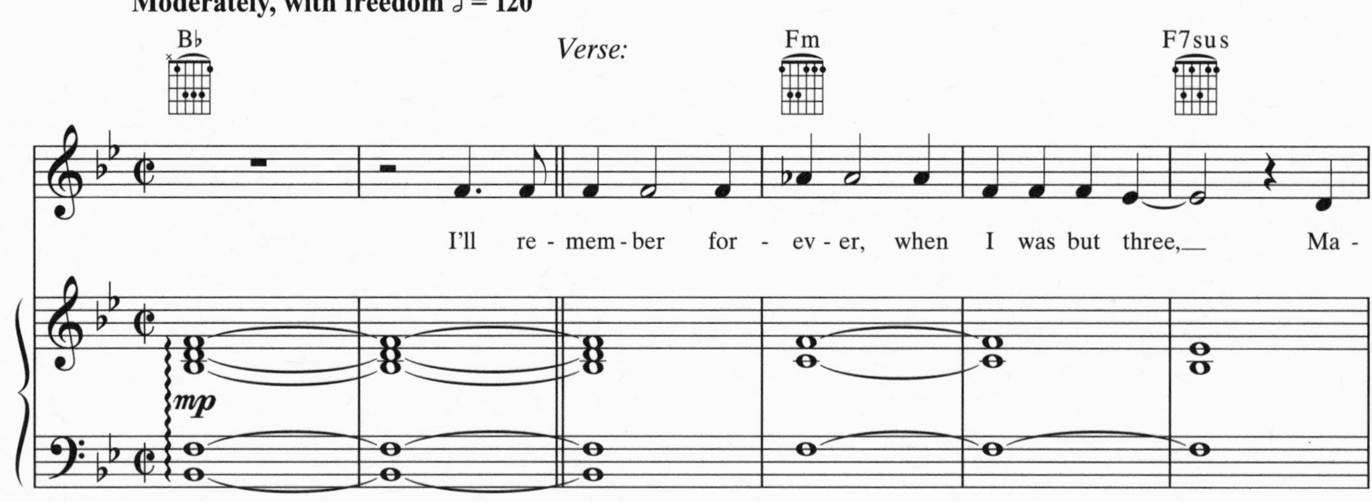

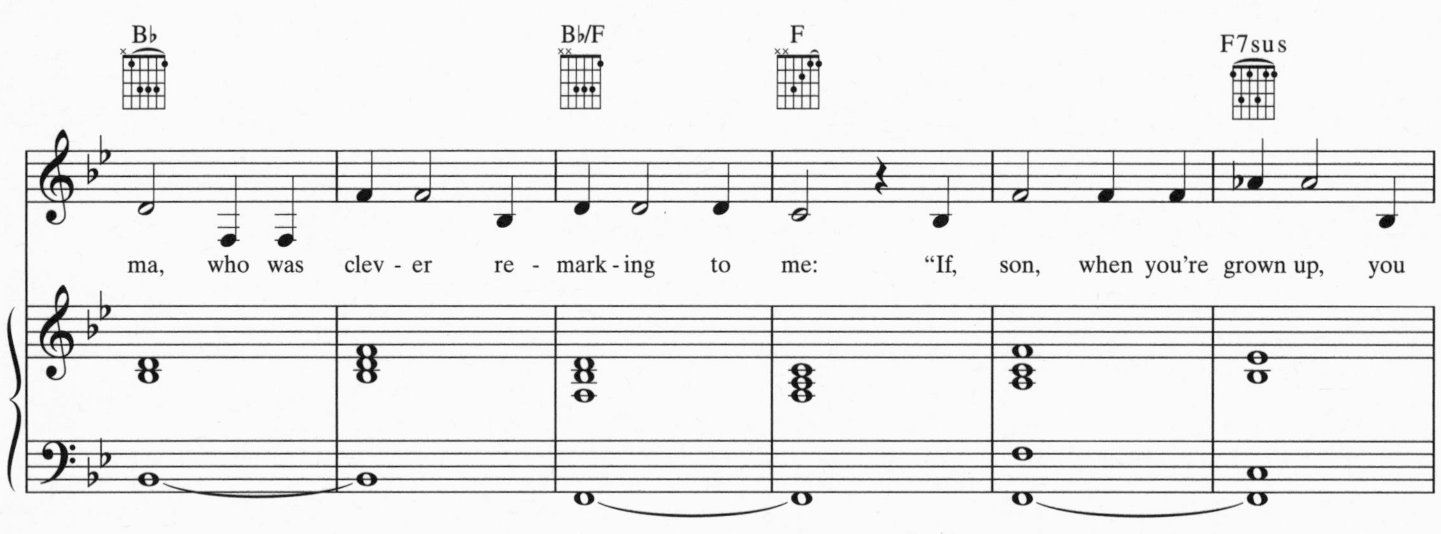

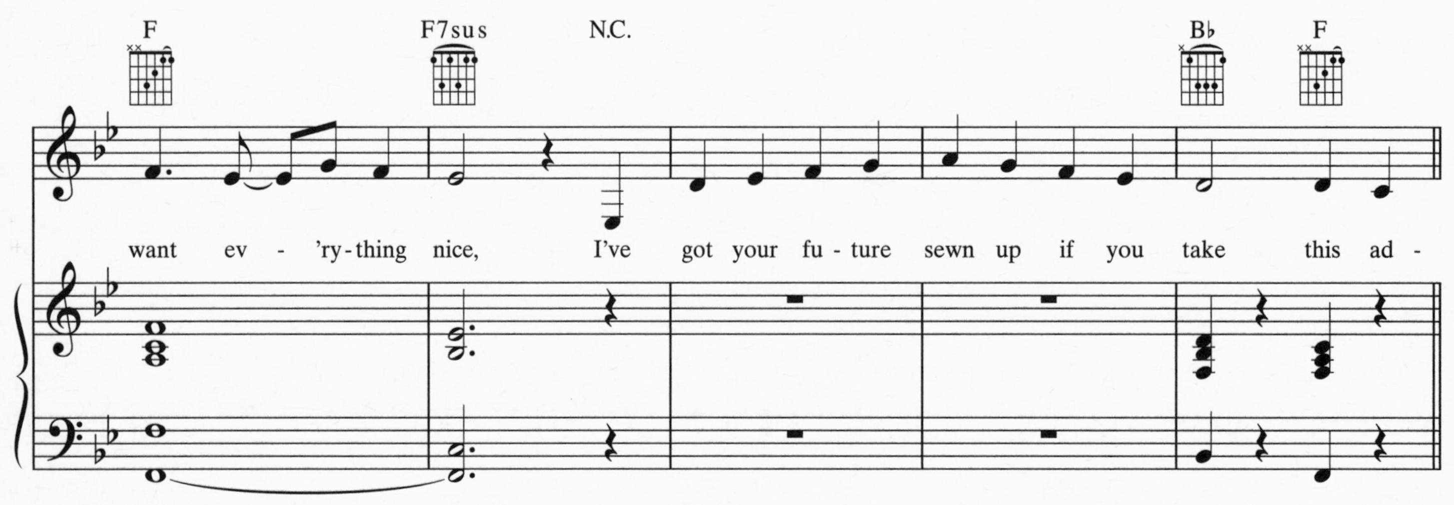

Fast ♩= 152
Refrain 1:
B♭ N.C.
B♭
Gm F7 B♭
Gm7 F Gm7
F C C7 F N.C.
vice: Be a clown!
Be a clown! All the world loves a
clown! Act the fool, play the calf
and you'll al - ways have the last laugh. Wear the

B♭
Gm
B♭7
cap and the bells and you'll rate with all
E♭6
F
B♭
F7
the great swells. If you be-come a doc-tor, folks-'ll
C♯dim7
F7/C
F7
B♭
F7/C
C♯dim7
F7/C
face you with dread. If you be-come a den-tist, they'll be glad when you're dead.
F7
B♭
G7
Cm
E♭m
E♭m6
You'll get a big-ger hand if you can stand on your head. Be a

Bb/F
F7
Bb
N.C.
clown! Be a clown! Be a clown! Be a
Refrain 2 & 3:
Bb
Gm
F7
Bb
clown! Be a clown! All the world loves a
clown! Be a clown! All the world loves a
Gm7
F
Gm7
clown! Show 'em tricks, tell 'em jokes
clown! If you just make 'em roar,
F
C
C7
F
N.C.
and you'll on - ly stop with top folks. Be a
watch your moun - te - bank ac - count soar. Wear a

B♭
Gm
crack jack - an - apes and they'll
paint - ed mus - tache and you're
B♭7
E♭6
F
im - i - tate you like apes. Why
sure to make a big splash. A
B♭
F7/C
C♯dim7
F7/C
F7
be a great com - pos - er with your rent in ar - rears? Why
col - lege ed - u - ca - tion I should nev - er pro - pose. A
B♭
F7/C
C♯dim7
F7/C
F7
be a ma - jor po - et and you'll owe it for years, when
bach - e - lor's de - gree won't e - ven keep you in clo'es. But

B♭ G7 Cm E♭m E♭m6 B♭/F
crowds 'll pay to gig - gle if you wig - gle your ears? Be a clown! Be a
mil - lions you will win if you can spin on your nose. Be a clown! Be a
F7 B♭ F9(♯5) B♭ G7
clown! Be a clown!
clown! Be a clown!
C7 F7 1. B♭6 N.C. 2. C7
Be a
G7 C7 F7 B♭6 N.C.
Give 'em

Refrain 4:
B♭
Gm
quips, give 'em fun and they'll
B♭7
E♭6
F
pay to say you're A - 1. If
B♭
F7/C
C♯dim7
F7/C
F7
you be - come a farm - er, you've the weath - er to buck. If
B♭
F7/C
C♯dim7
F7/C
F7
you be - come a gam - bler, you'll be stuck with your luck. But

B♭
G7
Cm
E♭m
Freely and Conducted
jack you'll nev - er lack if you can quack like a duck.
(Quack, quack, quack.)
rit.
N.C.
B♭/F
F
Be a clown! Be a clown!
N.C.
E♭/F
F7
B♭
F9(♯5)
Be a clown!"
a tempo
B♭
G7
C7
F7
B♭6 N.C.

LET'S DO IT, LET'S FALL IN LOVE

Words and Music by
COLE PORTER

Easy swing (𝅗𝅥 = 69)

G(9) D7 G C6 Cm6

best up - per sets do it, Lith - u - an - i - ans and Letts do it,

mf

Bm7 B♭9 Am7 D7 G C7 G N.C.

let's do it, let's fall in love. The Dutch in

Em Am7 Bm7 G7 G13

old Am - ster - dam do it, not to men - tion the Finns.

C F7 B♭ Am11 D9(♯5)

Folks in Si - am do it, think of Si - am - ese twins. Some Ar - gen -

G6 Am7 D7 G C7 Cm
tines, with-out means, do it, peo-ple say, in Bos-ton, e-ven beans do it,
Bm7 Em7 Am7 D7 G Cm G N.C.
let's do it, let's fall in love. 2. Ro-man-tic
Refrain:
G6 D7 G C Cm
spong-es, they say, do it, oys-ters, down in Oys-ter Bay, do it,
Bm7 B♭7 Am7 D7 G Em7 Am D9(♯5)
let's do it, let's fall in love. Cold Cape Cod
3
3

G D7 G C6 Cm6
clams, 'gainst their wish, do it, e - ven laz - y jel - ly - fish do it,
Bm7 B♭7 Am7 D7 G Cm G N.C.
lets' do it, let's fall in love. E - lec - tric
Em Am9 Bm7 G7
eels, I might add, do it, though it shocks 'em I know.
C F7 B♭ Am11 D9(♯5)
Why ask if shad do it, wait - er, bring me shad roe. In shal - low

G D7 G C7 Cm6
shoals, En-glish soles do it, gold-fish, in the pri-va-cy of bowls, do it,
Bm7 Em7 Am7(♭5) D7 G Cm G N.C.
let's do it, let's fall in love.
3. The dra-gon -
Refrain:
A6/9 Bm7 E7 A6 A13 D7 Dm6
flies, in the reeds, do it, sen-ti-men-tal cen-ti-pedes do it,
C♯m11 C9 Bm7 E9 A Dm6 A E9(♯5)
let's do it, let's fall in love. Mos-qui-toes,

A6 A+ A Bm7 E7 A6 D6 Dm
heav - en for - bid, do it, so does ev - 'ry ka - ty - did, do it,
C♯m7 C7 Bm7 E9 A Dm6 A N.C.
let's do it, let's fall in love. The most re -
rall.
Slow swing ♩ = 100
F♯m7 Bm7 C♯m7 A9
fined la - dy bugs do it when a gen - tle - man calls.
f
Dmaj7 G9 C Bm11 E9(♯5)
Moths in your rugs do it, what's the use of moth balls? Lo - custs in

A6
Bm7
E7(♭9)
A6
trees do it, bees do it, even over-educated
accel. poco a poco
Tempo segundo (𝅗𝅥 = 69)
D7
Dm
C♯m7
F♯m7
Bm7(♭5)
E7
A
Dm6
fleas do it, let's do it, let's fall in love.
C♯m7
F♯m7
Bm7
A/E
E7
A
Dm6
Let's do it, let's fall in love.
C♯m7
F♯m7
Bm7(♭5)
E7
A
Dm6
A
Let's do it, let's fall in love.

BEGIN THE BEGUINE

Words and Music by
COLE PORTER

Cm6
B♭
Am7(♭5)
brings back a night of trop - i - cal splen - dor, it
D7sus(♭9)
D7
Gm
D7(♭9 ♯5)
brings back a mem - 'ry ev - er green. I'm
Verse:
B♭6
D7sus(♭9)
Gm7/D
Cm7/D
with you once more un - der the stars, and
Gm/D
Gm11/D
D7sus(♭9)
D7
down by the shore an or - ches - tra's play - ing, and

Cm7/D
D7(♯5)
Cm7
Am7(♭5)
D7sus(♭9)
e - ven the palms seem to be sway - ing
D7
Gm7/D
D7sus(♭9)
when they be - gin the be - guine. To
Bridge:
Gm7
Cm9
F
live it a - gain is past all en - deav - or, ex -
Fm7
B♭7
E♭maj7
E♭6
cept when that tune clutch - es my heart, and

E♭7 D E♭
there we are, swear - ing to love for - ev - er, and prom - is - ing
D Cm7 D7(♭5) D7
nev - er, nev - er to part. What
Verse:
Gm/D D7sus(♭9) Gm7/D Cm/D
mo - ments di - vine, what rap - ture ser - ene, till
Gm/D B♭maj7 B♭7 Am7(♭5) D7
clouds came a - long to dis - perse the joys we had tast - ed, and

Cm6
Cm7
Am7(♭5)
D7(♭9)
now when I hear peo - ple curse the chance that was wast - ed,
I
D7sus(♭9)
D7
Gm7/D
F7/D
know but too well
what they
mean;
so don't
Chorus:
B♭
Cm7/B♭
B♭
let them be - gin
the be - guine,
Cm7/B♭
B♭
F7/B♭
let the love that was once a fire re - main an

F
E♭maj7
D7
Cm
em - ber;
let it sleep like the dead de -
Am7(♭5)
Gm
E♭maj7
sire I on - ly re - mem - ber
Am7(♭5)
Cm9
B♭
F11
F7
when they be - gin the be - guine.
Oh yes,
Chorus:
B♭
Cm7/B♭
B♭
let them be - gin the be - guine, make them play

Cm7/B♭
B♭
F7/B♭
till the stars that were there be - fore re - turn a -
F
E♭maj7
D7
Cm7
bove you, till you whis - per to me once
Am7(♭5)
Gm
E♭maj7
more, dar - ling, I love you! And we
E♭maj7/A
D7
Am7(♭5)
sud - den - ly know what heav - en we're in,

D7sus(♭9)
D7
when they be - gin
the
Gm
Cm/G
Cm6/G
be - guine,
when they be - gin
Cm6
D7sus(♭9)
Gm7
D7sus(♭9)
the be - guine.
rall.
a tempo
B♭maj7
D7(♭9 ♯5)
Gm11
molto rit.

ANYTHING GOES

Words and Music by
COLE PORTER

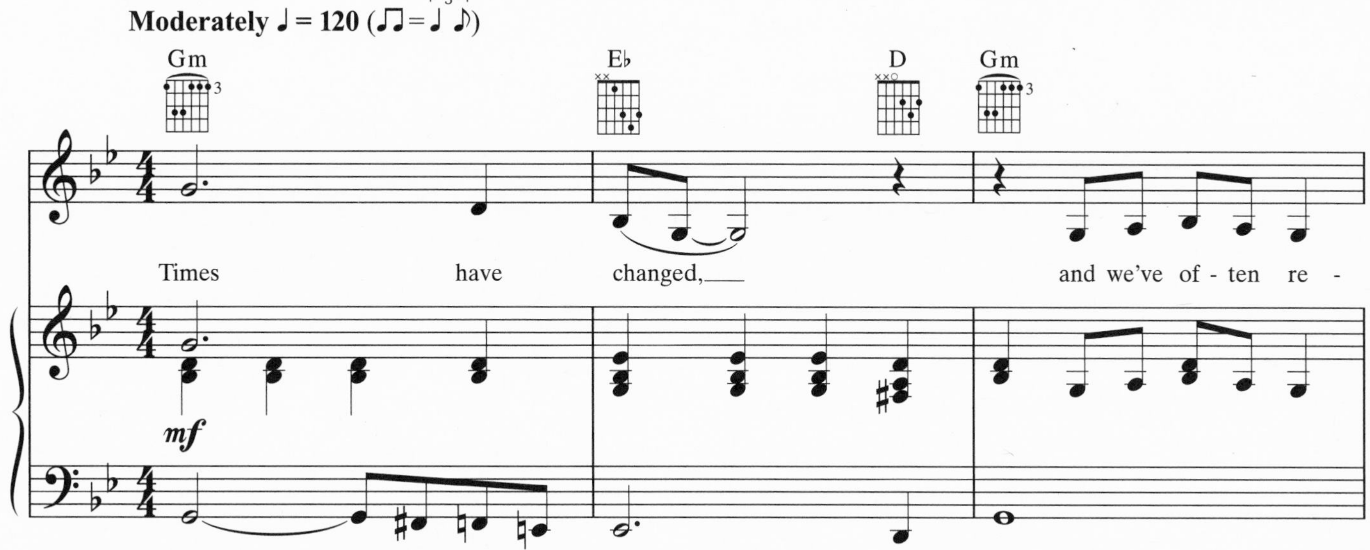

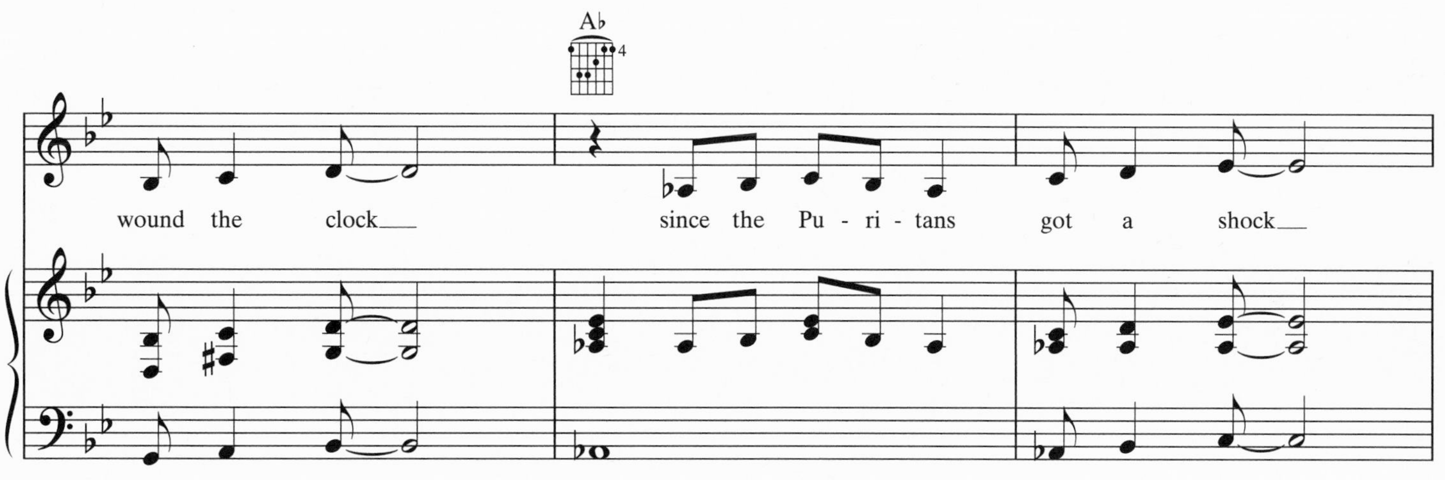

Cm
day,
an - y shock they should try to stem,
D7
Gm
D/A
A7
3
'stead of land - ing on Ply - mouth Rock,
Ply - mouth Rock would land on
D7
Brightly 𝅗𝅥 = 96
Refrain:
G
them.
In
old - en days, a
Gmaj7
G6
Em
G7
glimpse of stock - ing was looked on as some - thing shock - ing. Now, heav - en knows,

C
G/B
Am
Cm
G
an - y - thing goes.
D7
G
Gmaj7
Good au - thors, too, who once knew bet - ter words,
G6
Em
G7
C
G/B
now on - ly use four - let - ter words writ - ing prose.
Am
D7
G
F♯7
An - y - thing goes.
(Chorus:) (If say - ing your

Bm
F♯7
(Lead:) If say - ing your prayers you like, if green
prayers you like,) (if green pears you like,)
Bm
pears you like, if old chairs you like,
(if old chairs you like,) (if back
F♯7
Bm
if back stairs you like, if love af -
stairs you like,) (if love af - fairs you like)
D/A
G♯m7(♭5)
fairs you like with young bears you like, why, no -
(with young bears you like,) (All:)

G
D7
G
bod - y will op - pose.
So, though I'm not a
Gmaj7
G6
Em
G7
great ro - manc - er, I know that I'm bound to an - swer when you pro - pose.
C
G/B
Am
D7
G
An - y - thing goes.
F♯7
Bm
(Lead:) If driv - ing fast cars you like, and low
(Chorus:) (If driv - ing fast cars you like,)

F♯7
Bm
bars you like,
(and low bars you like,)
and old hymns you like,
(and old hymns you like,)
F♯7
if bare limbs you like,
(if bare limbs you like,)
if Mae
Bm
D/A
West you like,
(if Mae West you like,)
or me un - dressed you like,
(or me un - dressed you like,)
G♯m7(♭5)
G♯dim7
D7
(All:) why, no - bod - y will op - pose.
And

G
Gmaj7
G6
ev - 'ry night, the set that's smart__ is in - trud - ing on nud - ist par -
Em
G7
C
G/B
Am
D7
___ ties in stu - di - os.______ An - y - thing
G
Em
Am
D7
G
Em
goes. An - y - thing goes.
Am
Cm
G
An - y - thing goes.________________

I LOVE YOU

Words and Music by
COLE PORTER

Gm7(♭5)
C7
Fmaj7
Bm11
E7sus
love you," the gold - en dawn a - grees as once
2nd time - spoken: I do love you, darling.
Amaj7
F♯m7
Bm7
E7
Amaj7
more she sees daf - fo - dils.
A♭7(♯5)
Gm9
C7
(1.2.) It's spring a - gain and birds on the
...end solo)
cresc.
f
Fmaj7
Dm7
Am7(♭5)
wing a - gain start to sing a - gain

D7
Gm7
C7
Gm7(♭5)
the old melody.
"I love you,"
dim.
mf
C7
Am
D7
Gm7
that's the song of songs
and it all belongs to
1.
C13
F6
B♭m6
F6
you and me.
2.
C13
F6
B♭m6
F6
you and me.

SO IN LOVE

Words and Music by
COLE PORTER

*Original recording in key of E♭ minor.

Em
Am
I'm close to you, dear, the
D
D7(♭9)
G
G7
stars fill the sky, so in
C
F♯7(♭9)
B7
B7(♭9)
love with you am I.
Em
B7
E - ven with - out you, my

Em
Am
arms fold a - bout you. You
D
C/E
Cm/E♭
(unis.)
know, dar - ling, why; so in
G/D
G
love with you am I. You
C6
D7
G
Gmaj7
G6
G
(harmony 2nd time only)
(unis.)
love with the night mys - te - ri - ous, the

C6
D7
G6
night when you first were there.
In
C6
D7(♭9)
G
Gmaj7
G6
B7
(unis.)
love with my joy, de - lir - i - ous when I
Em
Bm/D
C♯m7(♭5)
F♯7
B7
knew that you would care.
So,
Em
B7
taunt me and hurt me, de -

To Coda
Em
Am
D
ceive me, de - sert me. I'm yours
D7/C
Bm7(♭5)
E7
Am
till I die, so in love,
Am7(♭5)
G/D
Gm/D
Gdim7
so in love, so in love with
D7sus
D7
C/D
G
D.S. al Coda
you, my love, am I. In

Coda
D7/C
Bm7(♭5)
E7
till I die, die, so in
rit.
Slower, deliberately ♩ = 104
Am
Am7(♭5)
G/D
Gm/D
love, so in love, so in love, so in love, so in
Gdim7
D7sus
D7
(unis.)
love with with you, my love am
rit.
G
Cm6
G
I.
8va
a tempo
rit. poco a poco

TRUE LOVE

Words and Music by
COLE PORTER

A♭
A♭m6
E♭/B♭
F9
Fm7
B♭7
far a - bove par; oh, how luck - y we are. While I
Refrain:
E♭
A♭
E♭dim7
E♭
B♭7
give to you and you give to me true
A♭
E♭
A♭
love, true love. So, on and on it will
E♭dim7
E♭
B♭7
al - ways be true love, true

E♭
A♭m7
D♭7
G♭
E♭9
love. For you and I have a guard - ian an - gel on
A♭m7
D♭7
G♭
B♭7
E♭
high with noth - ing to do but to give to
rit.
a tempo
A♭
E♭dim7
E♭
1.
B♭7
you and you give to me love for - ev - er
E♭
Fm
B♭
2.
B♭7
E♭
more. I love for - ev - er more.
rit.

LOVE FOR SALE

Words and Music by
COLE PORTER

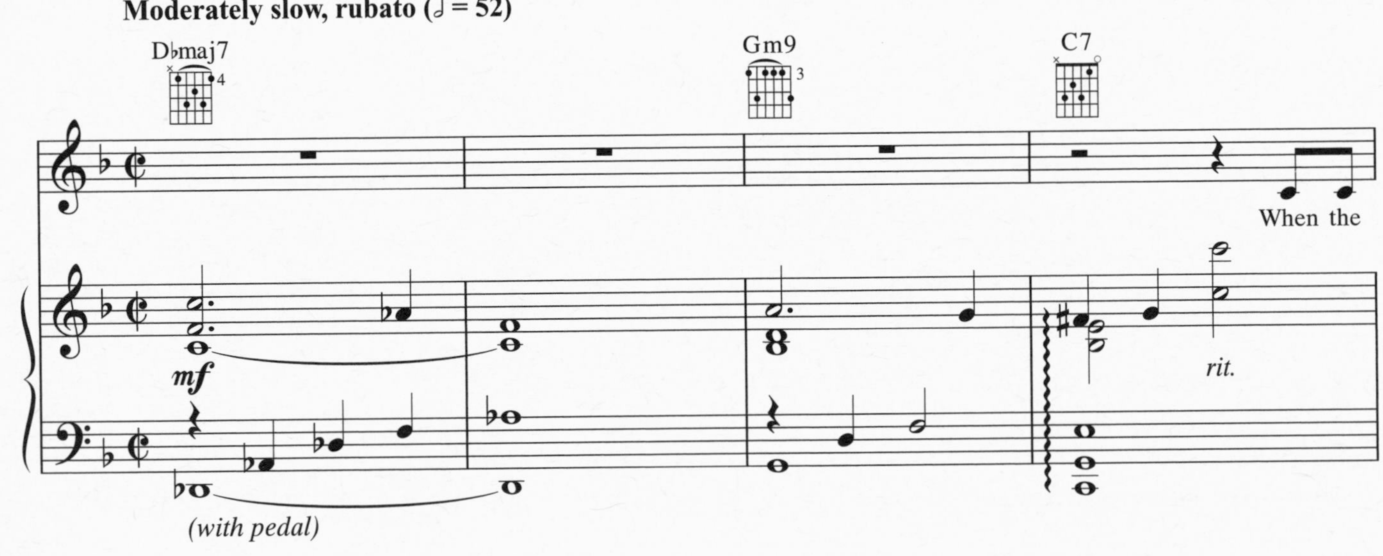

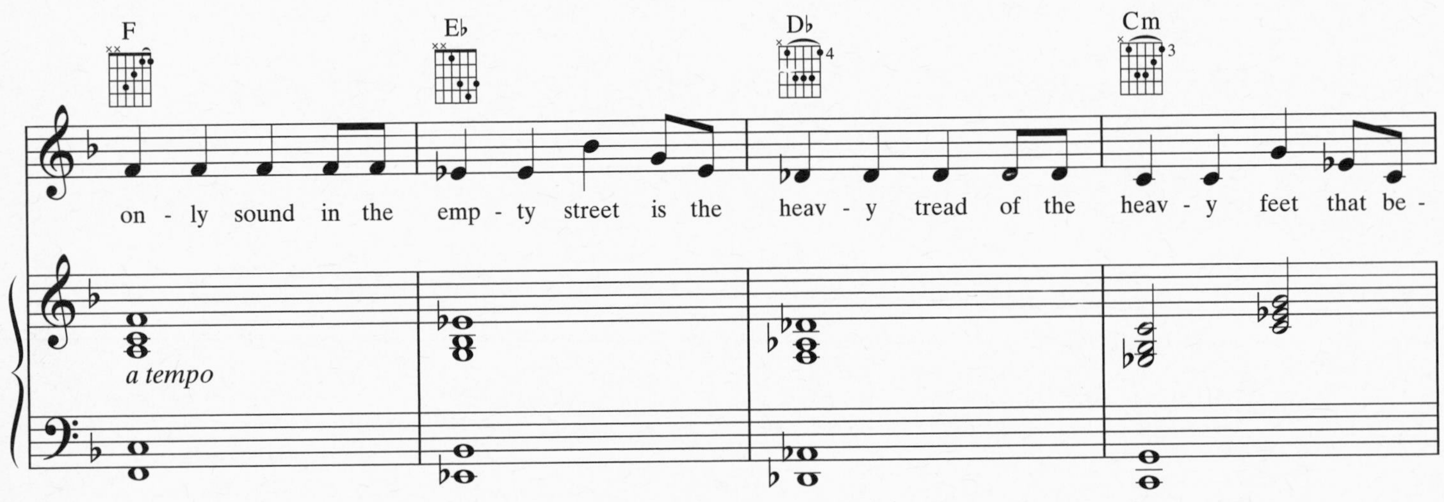

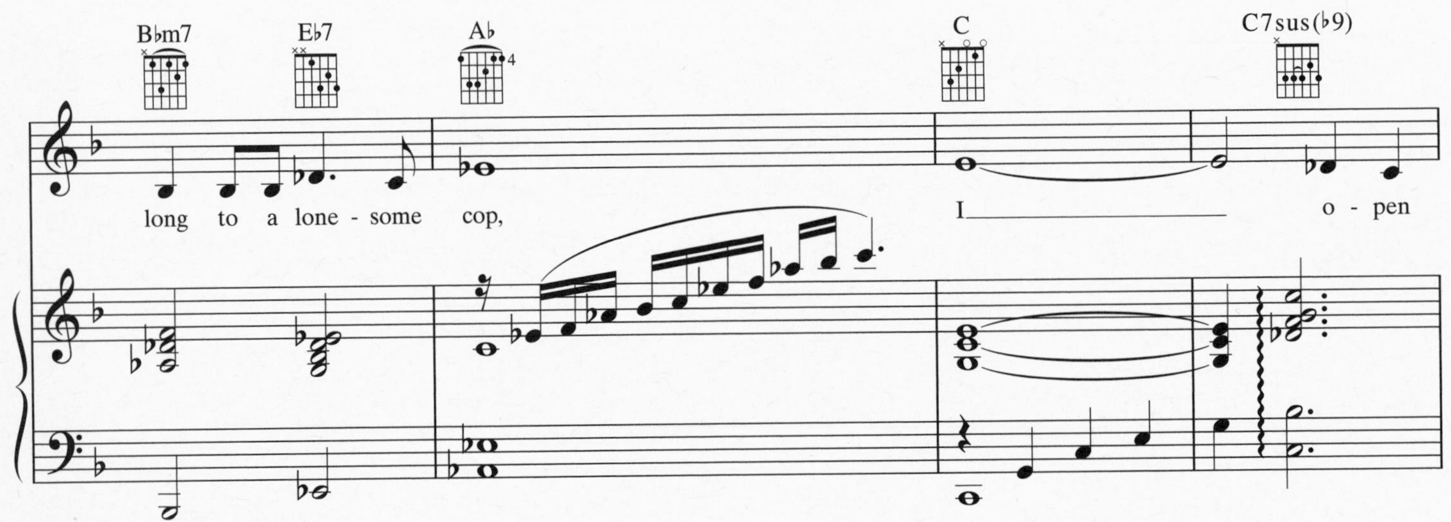

Fm
Gm7(♭5)
C7
F
E♭7
shop.
When the moon so long has been gaz - ing down on the
8va
D♭7
B13
E
E♭7
way-ward ways of this way - ward town that her smile be-comes a smirk,
8va
C
C7sus(♭9)
F
N.C.
I go to work.
(Drums)
3
Moderate swing ♩ = 104 (♫ = ♩♪)
3

B♭maj7
A♭13
8va
Refrain:
B♭maj7
A♭13
Love for sale,
3
B♭maj7
A♭13
ap - pe - tiz - ing young love for sale.
B♭m7
E♭7
A♭7
G♭7
Love that's fresh and still un - spoiled, love that's on - ly slight - ly soiled,

Gm11
G♭9(♭5)
Fm9
love
for
sale.
B♭maj7
A♭13
Who
will
buy?
B♭maj7
A♭13
Who would like to sam - ple my sup - ply?
B♭m7
E♭7
A♭7
D♭m9
G♭7
Who's pre-pared to pay the price for a trip to par - a - dise?

Gm11
G♭9(♭5)
Fm9
Love
for
sale.
B♭m7
E♭7
A♭maj7
Let the po - ets pipe of love in their child - ish
(2nd time Inst. solo ad lib.…
Cm7
B7
B♭m7
E♭7
way.
I know ev - 'ry type of love
A♭maj7
F7
bet - ter far than they.
If you want the

F7(♯5)
F7
B♭m7
thrill of love,
I've been through the mill of love;
Dm7(♭5)
G7sus(♭9)
G7
C♯m7(4)
F♯7
Cm7(♭5)
F7
old love, new love, ev - 'ry love but true love.
...end solo)
B♭maj7
A♭13
Love for sale,
B♭maj7
A♭13
ap - pe - tiz - ing young love for sale.

1.
B♭m7
E♭7
A♭maj7
D9(♭5)
D♭maj7
If you want to buy my wares, fol - low me and climb the stairs.
C7sus(♭9)
C7(♯5)
Fm9
D.S. 𝄋
Love for sale.
2.
A♭maj7
D9(♭5)
D♭maj7
Rubato, even eighths
fol - low me and climb the stairs. Love
rit.
8va
for sale.

WHAT IS THIS THING CALLED LOVE

Words and Music by
COLE PORTER

F♯
Am6
B7
E
win - dow,
I was so hap - py then.
But
A7
D/F♯
Dm/F
F7(♯11)
E7(♯5)
A
af - ter love had stayed a lit - tle while,
love flew out a - gain.
What
2 beat swing
Refrain:
Dm
is this thing called love?
E7
This fun - ny thing called

A
A7
love?
Just who can solve this
Dm
E7
mys - ter - y?
Why should it make a
A
A7
D7
fool of me?
I saw you there on won - der - ful
3
G
G7
F
day.
You took my heart and threw it a -
3

E
E7
A7
way.
That's why I ask the Lawd
Dm
in heav - en a - bove,
what
E7
1.
A
A6
is this thing called love?
What
2.
A6
love?

EASY TO LOVE

Words and Music by
COLE PORTER

Gm7
C7sus
C7
Fmaj7
A♭dim7
So worth the yearn - ing for.
Gm7
C7
Am
A♭dim7
So swell to keep ev-'ry home fire burn-ing for.
...end solo)
Gm
Cm
Gm
C7
We'd be so grand at the game,
1.
F/C
Gm7
C7
F
D7
so care-free to-geth-er that it does seem a shame if

Gm7
B♭m6
F/C
G♯dim7
A7
Dm7
you can't see your fu - ture with me,
Gm7
C13
F
Am7
D7(♭9)
'cause you'd be, oh, so eas - y to love.
2.
Rubato
Gm7
F
D7
Gm9
B♭m6
geth - er that it does seem a shame if you can't see your
molto rit.
F/C
A7
Gm7
C13
F
fu - ture with me, 'cause you'd be, oh, so eas - y to love.

NIGHT AND DAY

Words and Music by
COLE PORTER

Moderately ♩ = 120

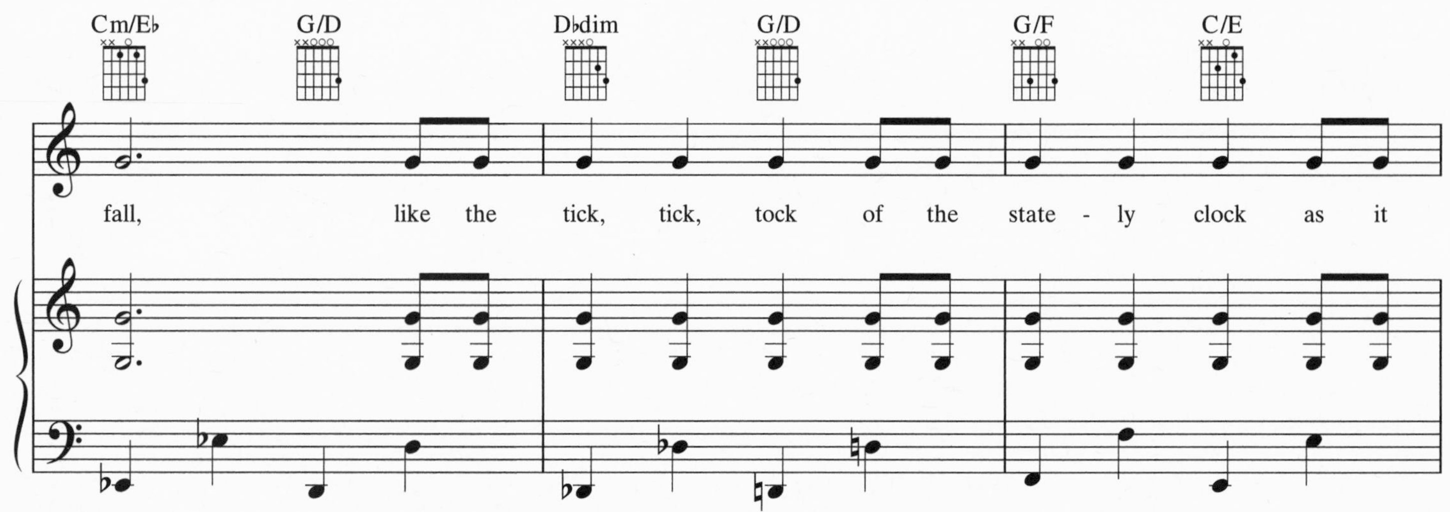

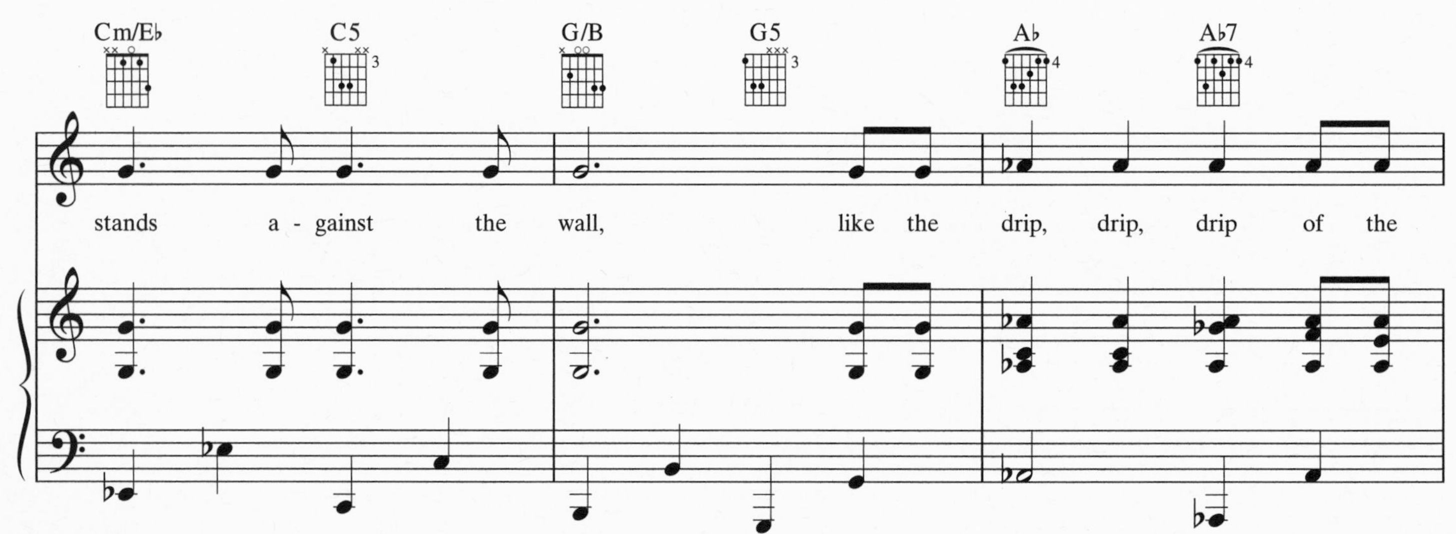

D♭/F D♭/A♭ A7 A5 D/F♯ Dm/F Fdim
rain - drops when the sum - mer show - er is through, so a
C/E Cm/E♭ G/D D♭dim C5 G/B Gm/B♭ G/A
voice with - in me keeps re - peat - ing, "You, you, you." Night and
rit.
Refrain:
A♭maj9 G7 Cmaj7 C6
day, you are the one. On - ly
a tempo
A♭maj9 G7 Cmaj7 C6
you be - neath the moon and un - der the sun. Wheth - er near

F♯m7(♭5)
Fm7
Em7
E♭m(maj7)
to me or far, it's no mat - ter, dar - ling, where you are, I
Dm
D+
G13
G7(♯5)
C6/9
B♭7sus
B♭7
think of you night and day. Day and
C♭maj7
B♭7
E♭maj7
night, why is it so, that this
C♭maj7
B♭7
E♭maj7
long - ing for you fol - lows wher - ev - er I go? In the

Am7(♭5)
A♭m7
Gm7
roar - ing traf - fic's boom, in the si - lence of my
G♭m(maj7)
Fm
B♭7
B♭7(♯5)
lone - ly room, I think of you night and
E♭6/9
G♭
day. Night and day, un - der the
8va
E♭
G♭
hide of me, there's an, oh, such a hun - gry

E♭
Am7(♭5)
yearn - ing burn - ing in - side of me.
And this tor - ment won't be
A♭m7
Gm7
G♭dim7
through 'til you let me spend my life mak - ing love to you
freely
Fm7(4)
B♭7sus
E♭
day and night, night and day.
a tempo
A♭m7
E♭6/9

LET'S MISBEHAVE

Words and Music by
COLE PORTER

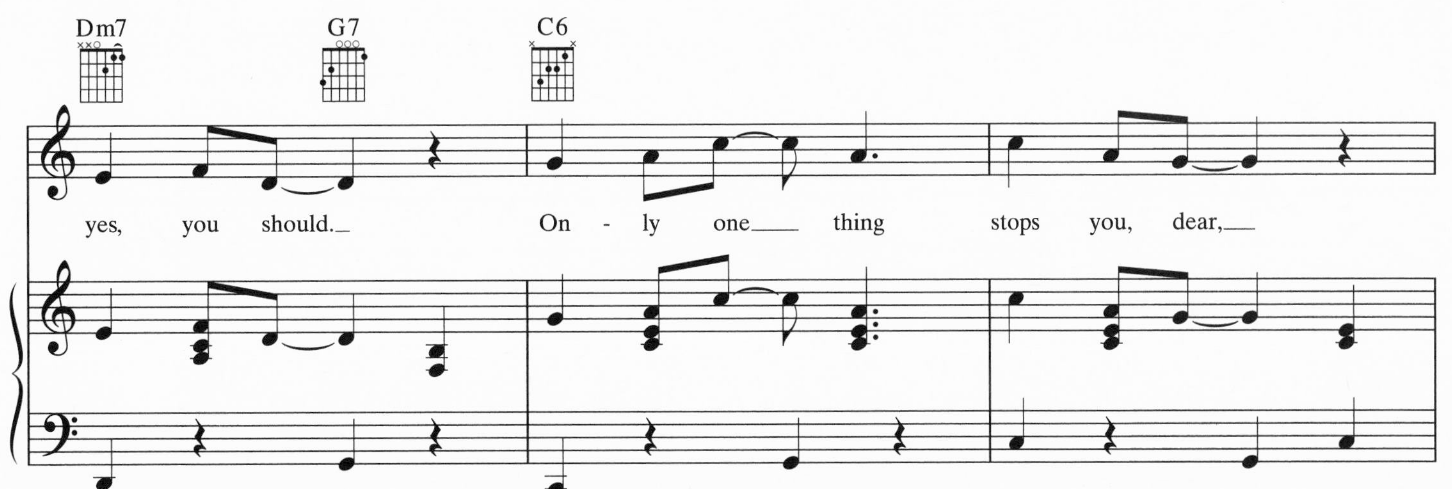

Dm7
G7
Dm7
G7
G♯dim
Am
Am/G
you're too good, way too good. If you want a fu -
F♯m7(♭5)
G9
Am
ture dar - ling, why don't you get a past?
C6
Dm7
G13
C
'Cause that fa - tal mo - ment's com - ing at last.
Refrain:
Am7
G7
C
G+
1. We're all a - lone; no chap - er - one can get our num -
2. See additional lyrics

C6
D7
ber, the world's in slum - ber,
G13
C
C/E
E♭dim7
Dm7
F♯
G
let's mis - be - have!
There's some - thing wild
C
G+
Am
a - bout you, child, that's so con - ta - gious,
Em
D7
let's be out - ra - geous, let's mis - be - have!

G7
F/A
A♯m6
G7/B
G7
C
C7sus
When A - dam won Eve's hand, he
C13
F6
Fmaj7
would - n't stand for teas - in', he did - n't care
D7
C/E
Fdim7
D7
G13
F/A
A♯dim
a - bout those ap - ples out of sea - son.
G/B
F♯7
G7
C
G9(♯5)
They say dat spring means just one thing to lit - tle love

To Coda 𝄌

C A7 D7 G13

birds, we're not a - bove birds; let's mis - be - have!

C

1. Dm G7

2. Dm7 G7

D.S. 𝄋 *al Coda*

2. It's get - ting late,

𝄌 *Coda*

G13 C G13 C

let's mis - be - have!

Verse 2:
It's getting late and while I wait,
My poor heart aches on,
Whey keep the brakes on?
Let's misbehave!
I feel quite sure, *un-peu d'a-mour*
Would be attractive,
While we're still active,
Let's misbehave!
You know my heart is true,
And you say, you for me care.
Somebody's sure to tell,
But what the heck do we care!
They say dat bears have love af-fairs
And even camels;
We're merely mammals,
Let's misbehave!

BLOW, GABRIEL, BLOW

Words and Music by
COLE PORTER

Moderate two-beat ♩ = 116

Eb/G
Fm7
Eb/G
bri - el play - in', Ga - bri - el, Ga - bri - el say - in',
Abm6 N.C.
Bb7
F7/C
Bb7/D
All:
"Will you be read - y to go when I blow my horn?" Oh,
Eb
Ab
Eb/G
Fm7
Eb
Ab
Eb/G
Fm7
blow, Ga - bri - el, blow! Go on and
Eb
Cm7
Fm7
Bb7sus
blow, Ga - bri - el, blow! I've

E♭
E♭7/G
A♭
Adim7
B♭7sus
been a sin-ner, I've been a scamp, but now I'm read-y to trim my lamp. So
E♭
A♭
E♭/G
Fm7
blow, Ga - bri - el, blow! I was
low, Ga - bri - el, low, might - y
Cm7
low, Ga - bri - el, low. But

E♭
E♭7/G
A♭
Adim7
B♭7sus
now, since I have seen the light, I'm good by day and I'm good by night. So
E♭
E♭7/G
A♭
B♭7sus
A♭
E♭/G
Fm7
G7
blow, Ga - bri - el, blow! Once, I
Cm
Fm/C
Cm
Fm
Cm
was head - ed for hell. Once, I
D7
G7
A♭7
A7
B♭7
was head - ed for hell. But

Eb
Eb7/G
Ab
Bb
when I got to Sa - tan's door, I heard you blow - in' on your horn once more, so
Cm
Fm7
G7(#5)
Cm
I said, "Sa - tan, fare - well." And now, you're
Fm7
C7
all read - y to fly, yes, to
Fm7
Ab
Eb
fly high - er and high - er and high - er. 'Cause you've

G♭ D♭
gone through the brim - stone and you've been through the fire. And you've
F F/A B♭7sus B♭6 B♭7sus B♭7
purged your soul and your heart, too, so climb up the moun - tain top and start to
E♭ A♭ E♭/G Fm7 E♭ A♭ E♭/G Fm7 E♭
blow, Ga - bri - el, blow! Go on and blow, Ga -
Cm7 Fm7 B♭7sus E♭ E♭7/G
bri - el, blow! I want to join your hap - py band and

A♭
Fm7
G7
Cm
A♭
B♭7
E♭
play all day in the Prom-ised Land. So blow, Ga - bri - el, blow!
E♭
A♭
E♭/G
Fm7
E♭
A♭
E♭/G
E♭
(Inst. solo ad lib....
Cm7
Fm7
B♭7sus
E♭
E♭7/G
A♭
F/A
B♭
Cm
A♭
B♭7sus
E♭
B♭7sus
E♭
B♭7sus
...end solo)
dim.

Eb Ab Eb/G Fm7 Eb Ab Eb/G Fm7 Eb Ab
Blow, Ga - bri - el, blow! Blow, Ga -
mp
Eb/G Fm7 Eb Ab Eb/G Fm7 Ab Eb/G Fm7 Bb7sus
bri - el, blow! Blow, Ga - bri - el,
cresc.
Fm7 Bb7sus Bb7 Eb Cm7 Fm7 Bb7sus
Lead:
blow! Blow, Ga - bri - el, blow, blow, blow! I
mf
Eb Eb7/G Ab Fm7 G7 Cm
All:
want to join your hap - py band and play all day in the Prom-ised Land. So blow, Ga -

A♭ B♭7 Cm A♭maj7 B♭7 A♭ E♭/G Fm7 B♭7sus
bri - el, blow! Blow, Ga - bri - el,
E♭ Cm7 B♭7sus A♭ E♭/G Fm7 B♭7sus E♭
blow! Blow, Ga - bri - el, blow!
Cm7 B♭7sus A♭ E♭/G Fm7 B♭7sus E♭ Cm7 B♭7sus
Blow, Ga - bri - el, blow!
A♭ E♭/G Fm7 B♭7sus Cm Fm7/C E♭
Blow, Ga - bri - el, blow!
rit.

IN THE STILL OF THE NIGHT

Words and Music by
COLE PORTER

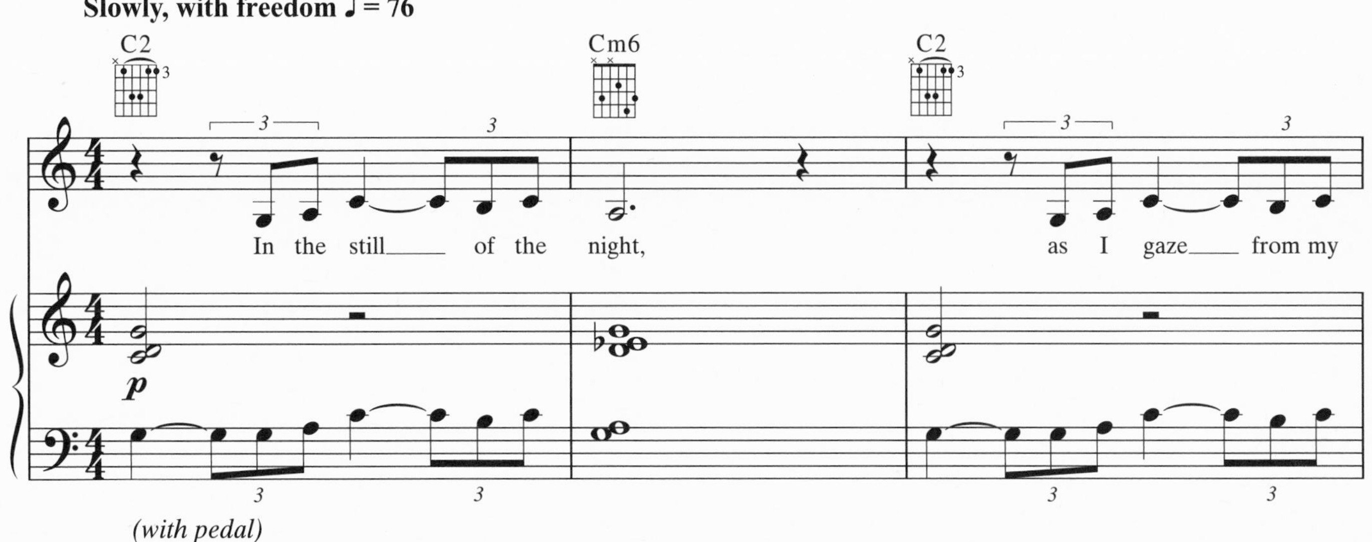

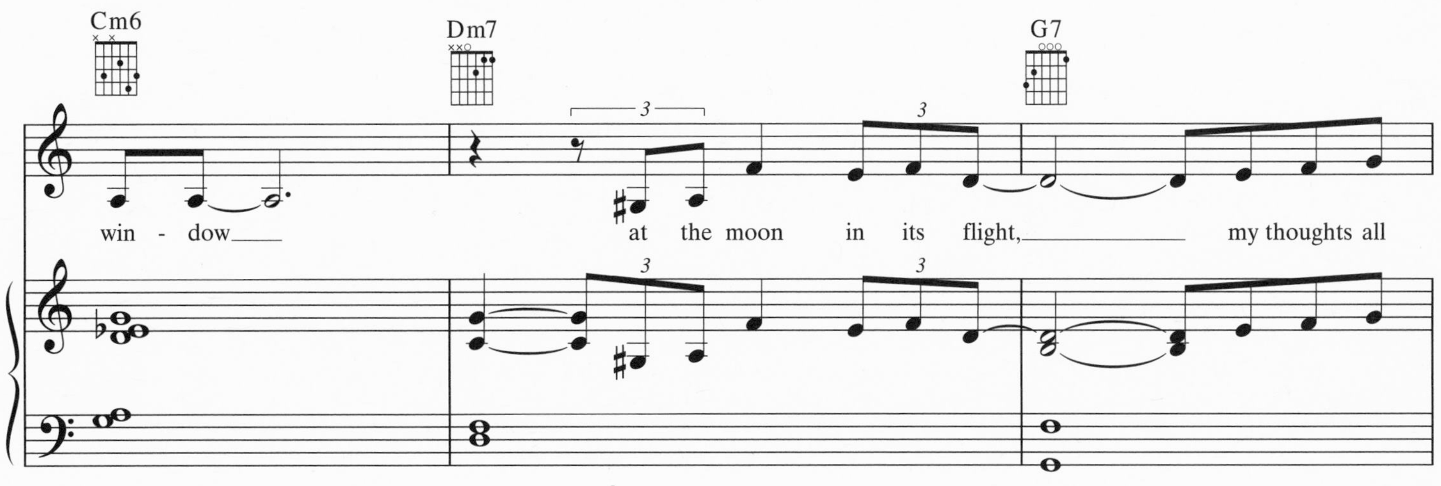

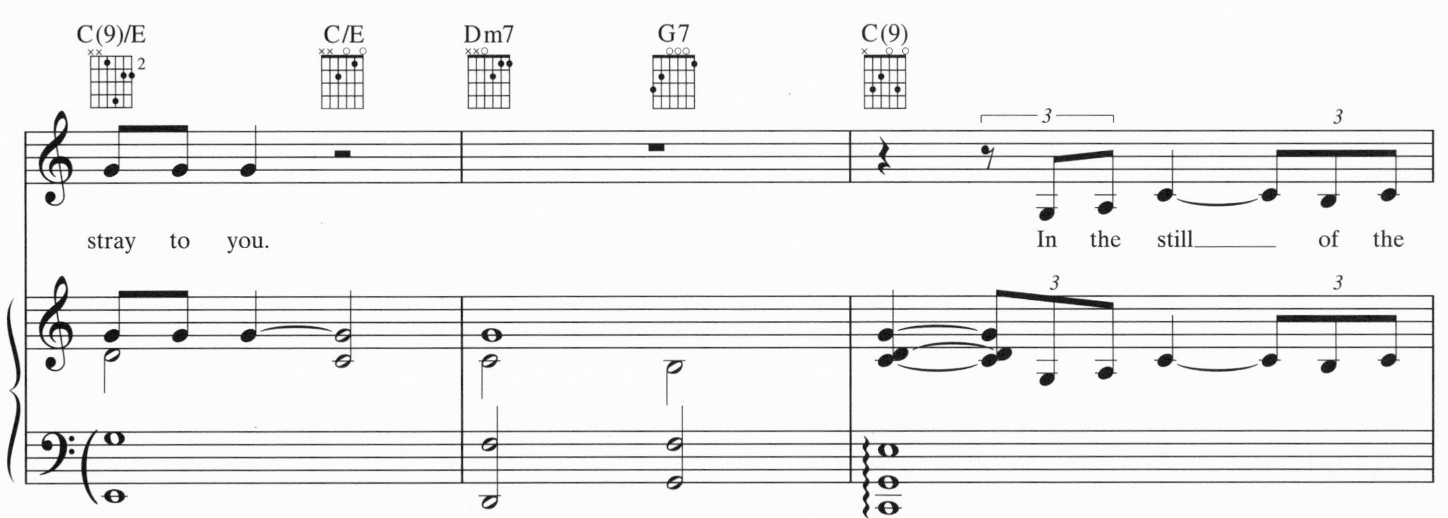

Cm6/9
C(9)
Cm6/9
B7
3
night, while the world is in slum - ber,
Em(9)
F♯m7
B7
Em
E♭dim7
3
oh, the times with-out num - ber, dar - ling, when I say to you:
Dm7
G7
C(9)
E7(♯5)
E7
Fmaj7
F6
2
"Do you love me
Dm7
G7
C(9)
C
C(9)
E7(♯5)
Fmaj7
F6
2
as I love you? Are you my life - to - be,

G7sus
G7
Em7(♭5)
A7
Dm7
my dream come true?"
Or will this dream of mine
Fm6/9
C(9)/E
F♯m7(♭5)
F6/9
3
fade out of sight
like the moon,
grow - ing dim,
on the
C(9)/E
E♭dim7
Dm7
G7sus
3
rim
of the hill
in the chill,
still
C
Cm6/9
C(9)
of the night?

YOU'RE THE TOP

Words and Music by
COLE PORTER

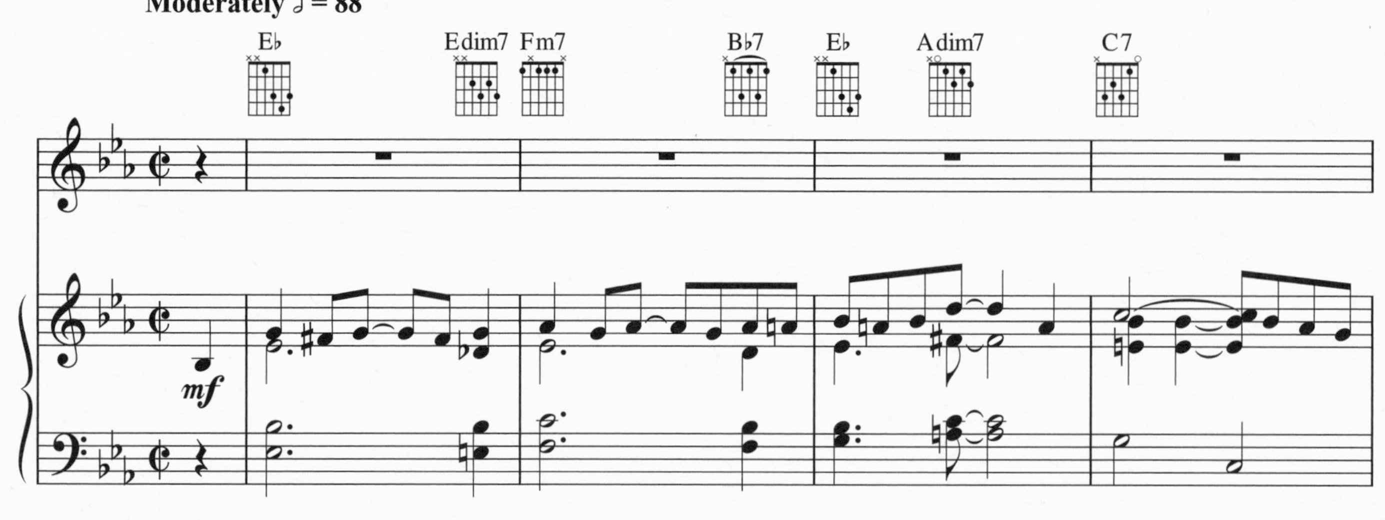

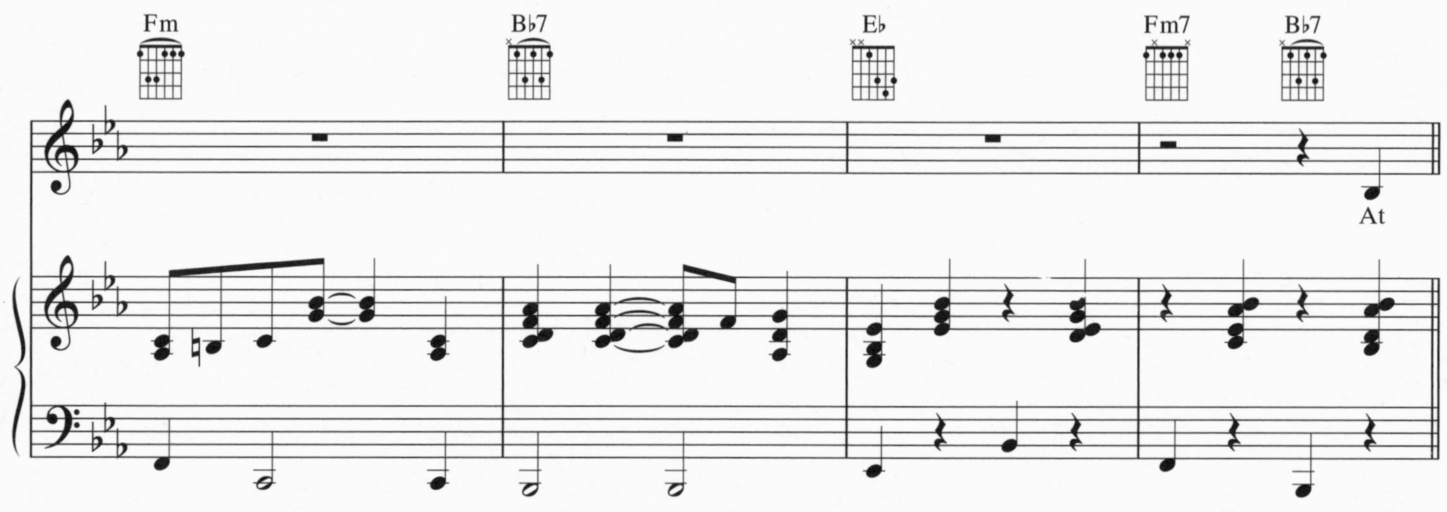

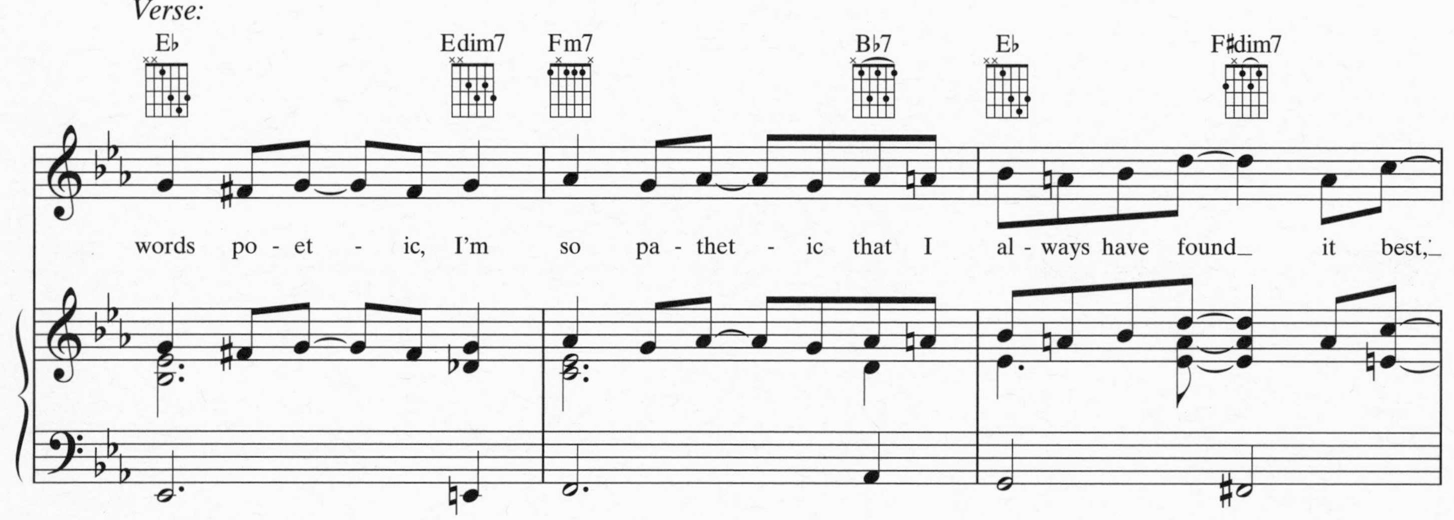

C7
Fm
B♭7
E♭
instead of getting it off my chest,
let it rest,
F7
B♭7
E♭
Edim7
Fm7
B♭7
unexpressed.
I hate parading my serenading, as I'll
E♭
Cm
D7
Gm
F♯dim7
probably miss a bar,
but if this ditty is
8vb
B♭/F
F7
B♭
N.C.
B♭9(♯5)
not so pretty, at least it'll tell you how great you are.

Refrain:
E♭
Edim7
B♭7
1. You're the top! You're the
2. You're the top! You're Ma -
3. You're the top! You're an
4. You're the top! You're a
E♭
Cm
Col - os - se - um. You're the top!
hat - ma Ghan - di. You're the top!
Ar - row col - lar. You're the top!
Wal - dorf sal - ad. You're the top!
G7
A♭
You're the Louvre Mu - se - um. You're a
You're Na - po - leon bran - dy. You're the
You're a Coo - lidge dol - lar. You're the
You're a Ber - lin bal - lad. You're the
Fm7
B♭7
E♭
B♭
mel - o - dy from a sym - pho - ny by
pur - ple light of a sum - mer night in
nim - ble tread of the feet of Fred As -
ba - by grand of a la - dy and a

Cm
D
Gm
Strauss.
Spain.
taire.
gent.
You're a Ben - del bon - net, a
You're the Na - tion'l Gal - l'ry, you're
You're an O - 'Neill dra - ma, you're
You're an old Dutch mas - ter, you're
C9
F13
B♭9
Edim7
B♭7
B♭9(♯5)
Shake - speare son - net, you're Mic - key Mouse.
Gar - bo's sal - 'ry, you're cel - lo - phane.
Whis - tler's ma - ma, you're Cam - em - bert.
Mrs. As - tor, you're Pep - so - dent.
E♭
You're the Nile.
You're sub - lime.
You're re - pose.
You're ro - mance.
You're the
You're a
You're In -
You're the
Tow'r of Pi - sa.
tur - key din - ner.
fer - no's Dan - te.
steppes of Rus - sia.
Cm
You're the smile
You're the time
You're the nose
You're the pants

E♭7
A♭
on the Mo - na Lis - a. I'm a
of the Der - by win - ner. I'm a
on the great Du - ran - te. I'm just
on a Rox - y ush - er. I'm a
Fm7
Gm7
A♭maj7
C7(♯5)
worth - less check, a to - tal wreck, a
toy bal - loon that's fat - ed soon to
in the way; as the French would say, "De
laz - y lout that's just a - bout to
F13
Fm7
Gm7
A♭
B♭7
flop,
pop,
trop,"
stop,
but if, ba - by, I'm the bot - tom, you're the
1.2.3.
4.
E♭
F♯dim7
Fm7
B♭7
B♭9(♯5)
E♭
top!
top!
8va
8vb